Icky, Sticky Slime!

by Ximena Hastings
illustrated by Alison Hawkins

Ready-to-Read

SIMON SPOTLIGHT
An imprint of Simon & Schuster Children's Publishing Division
New York   London   Toronto   Sydney   New Delhi
1230 Avenue of the Americas, New York, New York 10020
This Simon Spotlight edition May 2022
Text copyright © 2022 by Simon & Schuster, Inc.
Illustrations copyright © 2022 by Alison Hawkins • Stock photos by iStock
SIMON SPOTLIGHT, READY-TO-READ, and colophon are registered trademarks of Simon & Schuster, Inc.
For information about special discounts for bulk purchases, please contact Simon & Schuster Special Sales at 1-866-506-1949 or business@simonandschuster.com.
Manufactured in the United States of America 0322 LAK
2 4 6 8 10 9 7 5 3 1
This book has been cataloged by the Library of Congress.
ISBN 978-1-6659-1348-5 (hc) • ISBN 978-1-6659-1347-8 (pbk) • ISBN 978-1-6659-1349-2 (ebook)

Glossary

algae: a group of aquatic organisms that do not have roots, stems, or leaves.

antioxidants: substances that can help remove damaging effects from a living organism.

bacteria: one-celled organisms that can cause diseases.

mucus: a mixture of water, cells, and other things in the body that line the inside of the nose and other parts of the body to help protect them and keep them moist.

passion fruit: an edible fruit from a passionflower.

predators: living things that hunt, kill, and eat other living things.

saliva: a watery fluid in your mouth that helps you taste, chew, and swallow food.

Note to readers: Some of these words may have more than one definition. The definitions above match how these words are used in this book.

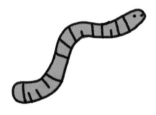

Contents

Chapter 1: The Scoop on Sticky Foods

Hi there! My name is Dr. Ick.
As my name suggests,
I like all things sticky, slimy,
and icky!
The stickier things are, the better!

This is my friend, Sam.
He doesn't love gross things
as much as I do.
We're here to share our knowledge
of all things ICKY, STICKY, and SLIMY!

There are a lot of slimy things
in the world.
And some of those
are foods that we eat every day!
Do you know what a very
sticky, slimy food is?
I'll give you a hint—it is a fruit.

Meet the **passion fruit**!
It is very nutritious and delicious,
and it is rich in healthy **antioxidants**
(say: an-tee-OCK-si-duhnts).
Do not let the slimy and sticky
texture inside the passion fruit
fool you!

Sometimes foods turn slimy on accident.
Take spinach, for example!

8

Spinach is mostly made up of water.
Once the spinach leaves start to age,
they turn into a green slime!

The leaves turn slimy because the
water is leaving the aged cells.

Here are some of the foods animals
depend on for survival.
Have you ever seen **algae** (say: AL-jee)
in the ocean? It is the slimy
green stuff that can wash up
on a beach during high tide.

Algae is a plant that lots of fish eat!
Giant kelp is the largest type of algae.
It can be more than two hundred
feet long!

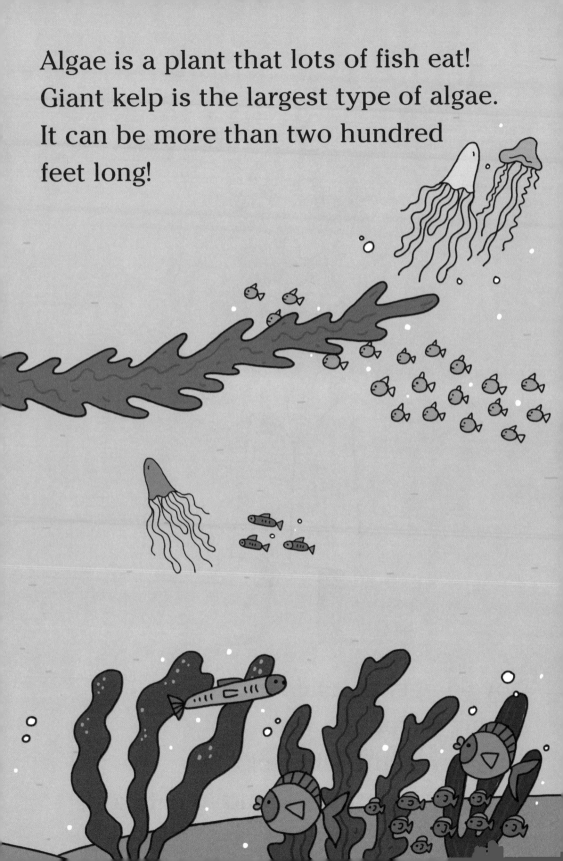

Chapter 2: Super Slimy Creatures

Speaking of animals, let me introduce you to a few of the slimiest, stickiest creatures found in nature!

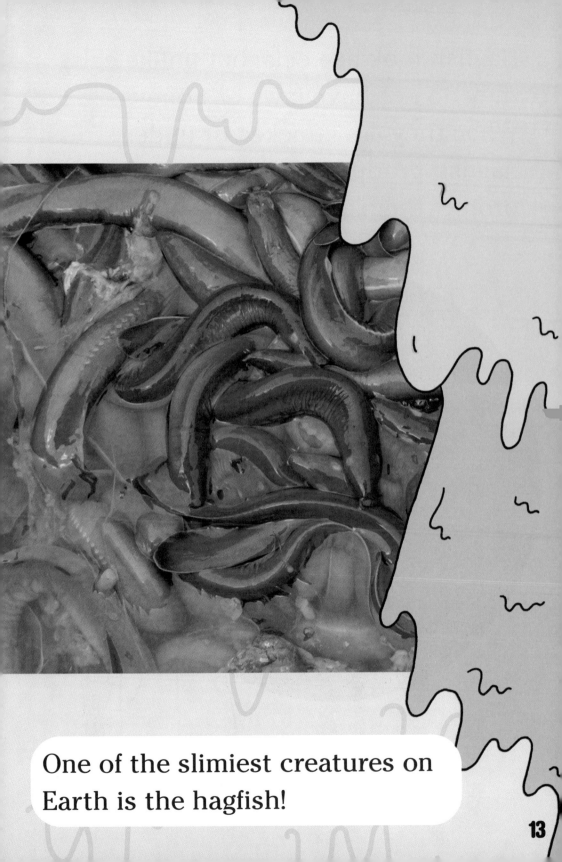

One of the slimiest creatures on Earth is the hagfish!

Hagfish look like eels, but unlike eels, they do not have jaws or bones. When they are attacked or under stress, hagfish produce snot-like slime to protect themselves.

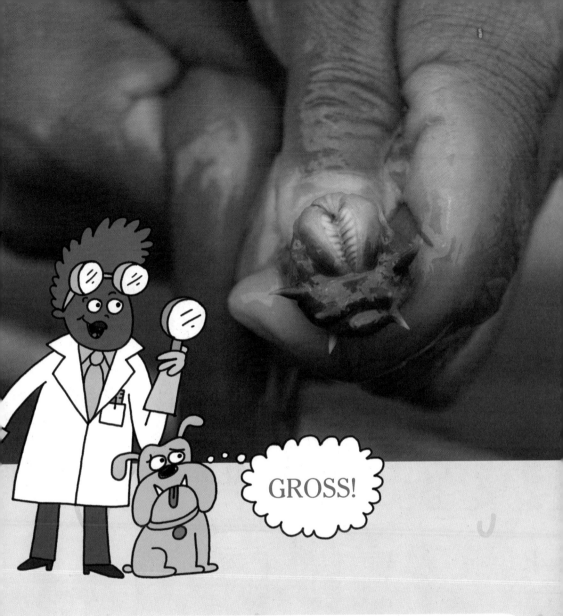

GROSS!

They can release a bucketful of slime in minutes!
When the hagfish releases slime, the slime combines with seawater and starts to expand!

Do you want to meet
a super sticky *and* super slimy
creature next?

You may have seen this one in
your backyard . . . the snail!

A snail releases **mucus** (say: myoo-kuhs) from glands inside their body, including their feet! The mucus from their feet allows snails to move over surfaces without hurting their bodies.

Unlike hagfish slime, snail slime can be *very* sticky.
Their slime also helps snails stick
to whatever surface they're moving on.
They can even travel upside-down!

Moving on to other creatures,
did you know there is a bird
that vomits on itself for protection?

It is the European roller.
When they feel threatened,
European roller chicks vomit
a smelly orange liquid on
themselves to scare off **predators**
(say: PRED-uh-ters).

Chapter 3: Icky, Sticky Body!

Now I want to introduce you to some of the sticky and slimy things inside your *own* body!

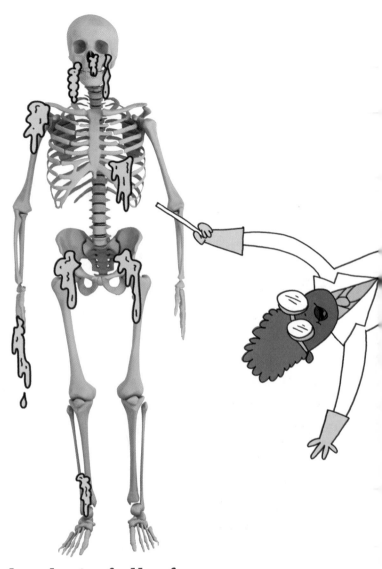

The human body is full of
mucus, **saliva** (say: suh-LIE-vuh),
and other slimy fluids!
In fact, humans have more than
twenty bodily fluids that
all have important jobs.

One of the fluids the body produces is also slimy. It's our mucus! Mucus is typically found in your lungs, mouth, and nose.

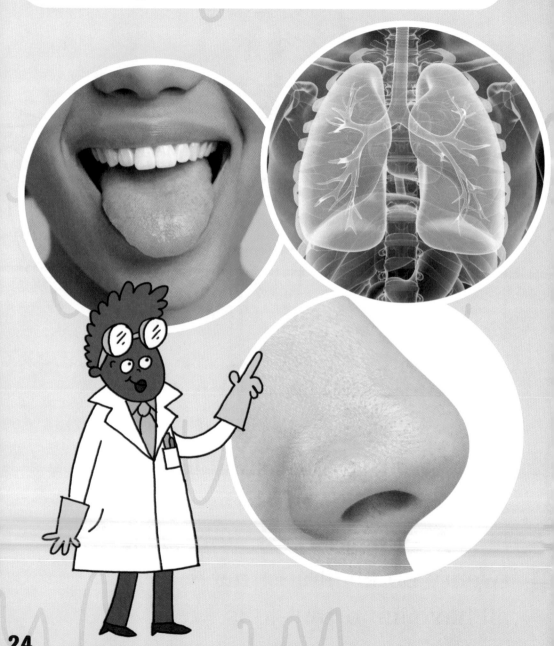

It is gross but also valuable, too.
Mucus traps unwanted germs,
and then the body flushes them out!

Humans produce
almost an entire
gallon of mucus
per day!

Boogers are just dry mucus.
Every time you blow your nose,
you're helping your body clean itself!

The color of mucus can also tell you a lot about what's going on inside your body. Next time you blow your nose, check out the color!

Clear: Normal mucus

Yellow/Green: You might be getting sick

Red: You may have a cut in your nose

Our bodies also create earwax! It can be dark yellow, or a grayish white. It is produced by glands in the ear canal.

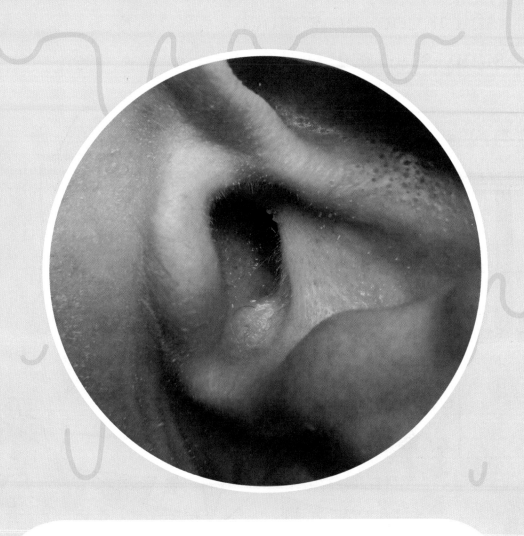

Like mucus, earwax traps **bacteria** (say: back-TEE-ree-uh).
Unlike mucus, you want to keep some earwax in your body because it helps protect your ears.

Isn't it cool how much slimy stuff exists?

Even though it's gross, it all
serves a purpose!
Long live the sticky, slimy, and icky!

Make Your Own Slime!

Want even more slime?
Create your own!
**Make sure to ask a
grown-up for help!**

You will need:

- glue
- baking soda
- plastic bowl

- saline solution
- liquid food coloring

Directions:

1. Pour an entire 4-ounce bottle of glue into a bowl.
2. Add a ½ tablespoon of baking soda to the bowl.
3. Add a ¼ tablespoon of saline solution.
4. Add a few drops of food coloring in any color you like!
5. Mix everything together. If it's too sticky, add a bit more saline solution.

Have fun playing with your icky, sticky slime!